Your Official America Online® Guide to Personal Computing

Your Official America Online® Guide to Personal Computing

Keith Underdahl

AOLPress ®

Dulles, VA

Your Official America Online® Guide to Personal Computing

Published by

AOL Press

An imprint of IDG Books Worldwide, Inc.

An International Data Group Company

919 E. Hillsdale Blvd., Suite 300

Foster City, CA 94404

www.aol.com (America Online Web site)

Library of Congress Control Number: 00-110868

ISBN: 0-7645-0837-7

Printed in the United States of America

10 9 8 7 6 5 4 3 2 1

1B/SY/QS/QR/IN

Distributed in the United States by IDG Books Worldwide, Inc. and America Online, Inc.

For general information on IDG Books Worldwide's books in the U.S., please call our Consumer Customer Service department at 800-762-2974. For reseller information, including discounts and premium sales, please call our Reseller Customer Service department at 800-434-3422.

 is a trademark
of America Online, Inc.

 is a registered trademark or trademark under exclusive license to IDG Books Worldwide, Inc. from International Data Group, Inc. in the United States and/or other countries.